D0111659

Lions and Tigers and Bears—Oh My

A Parable Concerning Diversity and Inclusion

By

Art Jackson

ISBN: 1-4107-3664-4 (softcover)
ISBN: 1-4107-3663-6 (electronic)

Library of Congress Control Number: 2003092011

This book is printed on acid free paper.

Printed in the United States of America
Bloomington, IN

1st Books - rev. 03/20/03

Lions and Tigers and Bears is a parable written to cause introspection and challenge beliefs concerning our diversity and how it impacts relationships and social intercourse. It is a tale of a mythical kingdom that is experiencing profound changes and how the inhabitants of that kingdom adjust and profit from their assets or resist and experience loss.

As understanding is required, guidance is sought from a wise one called 'The Teacher'. However a paradigm in thinking and beliefs is facilitated through profound insights gained from deep contemplation. We invite you to participate in the same process. Read and contemplate. Consider what you truly believe and why. We believe when you consider and truly understand the profound truths hidden in this parable, you can discover for yourself how to apply them to your situation so that you can profit from the diverse environment you exist in.

Written to evoke thought and the questioning of preconceived notions, the story takes a short amount of time to read ... but possible a lifetime to understand and implement. In an increasingly complex, sophisticated and global marketplace, we cannot succeed unless we attract top-caliber people that can provide the cultural and biological diversity we need to compete. To do less is to show up low on assets.

The author, Art Jackson Art Jackson is a graduate of the United States Military Academy at West Point and Lesley College in Cambridge, Massachusetts. Art holds a Bachelor of Science degree in Engineering, a Master of Science degree in Management and is continuing his studies towards a Master of Theology degree.

Art has been a speaker and trainer in Korea, Canada, Japan, Egypt and all across the United States delivering seminars on personal leadership, team building and diversity and inclusion. He has presented keynote addresses for Fortune 500 companies, government agencies, churches and schools.

Mr. Jackson brings a new perspective to diversity and inclusion work. His military background brings a very focused perspective that keeps him looking at two things. Mission first - People always. It is the mission that is most important and anything that gets in the way of the mission is to be overcome by any means necessary. People are the means by which the mission is accomplished, so any barrier to people performing at their very best is to be overcome by any means necessary. To the question, "which is most important, the mission or the people?", Art's answer is always "yes." The mission can not be accomplished without the people. And people can only prosper when the mission is accomplished. When we look at equal employment opportunity, affirmative action, diversity and inclusion from that prospective, we will se that everyone must play and play well. Everyone must use their own unique capabilities to maximum advantage to get the mission accomplished. Everyone must profit from the accomplishment of the mission.

Mr. Jackson is a member of the National Speakers Association, the National Capital Speakers Association, and the Les Brown 2000 Organization.

Please visit our web site at:

http://www.artjackson.com

Praise for Art Jackson Seminars

Presentations That Encourage And Promote
Personal Leadership To Allow Individuals And
Organizations To Manifest Their Intended Level
Of Greatness

Mounting Up On Wings Of Greatness
Purpose Centered Personal Leadership

"The most usable idea I gained from the seminar?
I can make a difference! You inspire me to be
more."
Sara Rosenkranz   Airline Reporting Corporation

Mounting Up On Wings Of Greatness
Purpose Centered Leadership For Leaders

"That was great! You've made a difference in the
way we see our practice site and how we can
change things"
Jessika C. Chinn   APhA-ASP President

Lions and Tigers and Bears
Profiting From Diversity Through Inclusion

"Not only is Art informative and entertaining, but attending his presentation has the possibility of saving your immortal soul!"

John Hunt   Office For Civil Rights
         Health and Human Services

Mounting Up On Wings Of Greatness
Team Building For Results

"Art is a dynamic speaker who focuses on the individual and the inherent potential that is in each of us."

Helen Sommerville National Air and Space Museum, Washington D.C.

Also …

"Art, you obviously touched people. The response to you was incredible as always."

Jo Condrill   President, GoalMinds

"I had heard you were a good speaker, but this was far beyond good. You helped me dream!"

Michael Southers President, Spiritual Fitness, Inc

Art Jackson Seminars presentations have been used by leaders in a myriad of personal and public interests to include:

Boston Univ., Boston, Ma.

Honeywell Electro Optics, Lexington, MA.

Loral Infrared & Imaging Systems, Lexington, MA.

U.S. Postal Service, Wash. D.C.

Federal Trade Commission, Wash. D.C.

Strayer University, Woodbridge, VA.

U.S. Equal Employment Opportunity Comm., Wash. D.C.

Equal Employment Opportunity Office, The Pentagon, Wash. D.C.

National Air and Space Museum, Wash. D.C.

The Learning Annex, Wash. D.C.

American Pharmaceutical Assoc., Wash. D.C.

Natl. Assoc. Of Chain Drug Stores, Wash. D.C.

DuPont Pharmaceuticals, Wilmington, DE

St. Mary's College, Maryland

St. John's Univ., New York, NY

Ft. Belvoir, VA

U.S. Office of Personnel Management

U.S. Department of Defense, The Pentagon

McKesson HBOC

GRC International Inc.

This work is dedicated to...

God ... who is the author and finisher of my faith.

Kim ... who believes in me when I need it most and reminds me that she'll let me know when it's time to worry.

Jennifer ... who keeps me confident that I can accomplish difficult things by being "high maintenance."

Family and friends ... who give me the desire to manifest greatness.

Ron Martin ... who got me interested in adapting my previous work to meet the needs of a diverse workforce (and threatened to kill me if he wasn't included on this page).

Contents

In Any Particular Situation ...

Each of us will find ourselves cast in the role of Lion ... or Tiger ... or maybe even Bear. The Kingdom presented in this story is inhabited by four categories of beings.

The Lions who have authentic or perceived power and authority.

The Tigers who have some perceived power simply because they look similar to Lions.

The Bears who have no power simply because they are so very different from Lions or Tigers.

The Hunters who represent a very real threat or difficulty.

And all of these beings are representations of all of us regardless of:

Culture	Gender	Age
Values	Ethnicity	Sexual Orientation
Personality	Spirituality	Habits and Customs
Physical Challenges	Education	Mental Challenges

Sometimes and in certain situations, we have power and authority. The ability to control and influence. And at other times, we are impacted by the power and authority held by others.

"sometimes you're the windshield ... sometimes you're the bug!"

The Development Of The Parable

This parable, as simple as it is was developed to address some very complex and important objectives.

To educate ourselves concerning the creation and maintenance of inclusive workplaces.

To cause contemplation resulting in the development of tools to support the encouragement of inclusive work environments.

To rededicate ourselves to integrate the inherent value of each individual's unique performance position into the fabric of all of our interactions

Phillip Keller wrote "Our Lord Himself, when He was amongst us, continually used natural phenomena to explain supernatural truth in His parables. It is a sound indisputable method both scientifically and spiritually valid. To understand one is to grasp the parallel principle in the other."

It was for this reason that I chose to present these ideas as a parable. But also it is hoped that as you read, you will through deep contemplation just like a certain Lion start to reevaluate some of your beliefs and determine for yourself which ones need modification. I would ask that you as the reader seek to find your own lessons herein as did the Lions, the Tigers and the Bears.

Lions

and Tigers

and Bears

Oh My

The Parable

The Kingdom

The Jungle

And it came to pass that there existed a kingdom inhabited by Lions and Tigers and Bears. Oh My! The Kingdom was composed of a thick jungle and a plain. To the far north, there were mountains. The jungle was thick with vegetation. There were waterfalls and rivers that teemed with all kinds of fish. The Lions and Tigers and Bears would often gather at the watering holes that were all around the kingdom.

In the jungle there were caves that were used as homes by all the inhabitants. From each cave could be heard the sounds of families being raised. Young Lions and Tigers and Bears growing up and eventually becoming adults in the three basic, and very separate communities.

The days were long and hot. But the evenings were most often cool. The air was filled with great multitudes of birds of every variety. On some days, there were so many birds in the sky that the sun was almost blocked out. They cast a great shadow across the ground. The kingdom was a wonderful place to be. Especially if you were a Lion ... or a Tiger ... or a Bear.

The Inhabitants

The inhabitants maintained a peaceful coexistence. There were seldom arguments and disagreements among them. Now there were almost never problems between the three groups mainly because there was seldom any contact between the Lions or Tigers or Bears. Each group had a separate culture that they were very proud of. They believed that they should be completely tolerant of those who were 'not like them'.

Lions and Tigers and Bears lived complete, full lives separated from each other. There had been times in the past when, because of a mutual problem they had to cooperate with each other. They always considered it a complete success when they worked well together but they also considered it extremely difficult and not worth any effort after the mutual problem had been resolved.

Chief among the Lions were Nono (no' – no) and Tau (tah' – oo). Nono was highly esteemed among the inhabitants of his pride and so he had the name. All the Lions desired to have the name because with the name came the ability to command great respect. The one who had the name led not only the Lions but also the Tigers and the Bears. So even though there was much desire to be the first among many, Nono had the name in the northern pride.

Tau had the name among the southern pride. His father had had the name before him and it was accepted that one day, Tau's son would have the name. Tau was well known for his ability to decide difficult situations and to take action. Tau could be counted upon to do what was best for all the inhabitants of the southern part of the jungle. By his actions, Tau was known for his virtue and just dealing. Tau had the name.

Both Tau and Nono were known for their courage in the face of great danger. They had kept their head when all others were losing theirs. When brush fires had swept the jungle, Tau and Nono had kept their calm. When drought made the jungle inhabitants fearful, these two remained steadfast. There were many Lions in the jungle, but Tau and Nono … they had the name.

There were large groups of Tigers that roamed through the jungle. The Tigers were led by Mpasa (em – pah' – sah). Mpasa was one of the most beautiful Tigers ever seen. His coat was thick and had an almost golden color. His claws were long and sharp. When there was a need to work with Lions or Bears, it was always Mpasa that stood for the Tigers. Mpasa was large and known to be the fiercest among the Tigers. His wisdom was highly esteemed among the Tigers. He had distinguished himself in combat time and time again. Mpasa had the name among all the Tigers.

There were also huge groups of bears led by one called Ebo (ee' – bo). Ebo had been given his name because of his great size. Even as a young bear, Ebo was large. He weighed many hundreds of pounds and had a large lumbering, yet powerful appearance. Ebo was one of the principal hunters among the bears. He had early learned to fish the streams and rivers that ran through the kingdom. Even when food was scarce in times of drought, Ebo could be counted upon to return to the caves inhabited by the bears with enough game to feed all that had failed during the hunt.

Ebo was well respected for his ability to reason through problems and come to a solution that would help all concerned. When ever difficult decisions were needed, all the bears, even those that were older would sit and await the word of Ebo. It was Ebo that had the name among the Bears.

But esteemed among all the inhabitants of the kingdom was Camara (cah – mah' – rah). Camara was a Lion but one who was revered for his great wisdom. Camara was old but still walked with great dignity. Younger Lions stepped aside when Camara came down the trail. Camara did not have to be present in any discussion and yet all there knew that it would be unwise to make any final decision without counsel from Camara.

Camara had long ago gained the nickname 'The Teacher'. Lions and Tigers and Bears sought Camara for his wisdom. As a matter of fact, Nono, Tau, Mpasa and Ebo had gained much of their wisdom and courage from the teachings of Camara. He was seen as a great resource for the entire kingdom.

The Hunters

The kingdom was a marvelous place to live except for one ever-present problem. The Hunters. The Hunters were humans that lived on the plains surrounding the jungle. They made their living and got their food from the things they found in the jungle. But they were most feared by the Lions and Tigers and Bears because they had for many years made their living by selling the meat and hides they harvested when they hunted Lions and Tigers and Bears. Oh My.

The Hunters had built their huts surrounding the jungle so they could be ever ready to take the unsuspecting Lion or Tiger or Bear that might wander too close to the edge of the jungle. There was no way out of the jungle without passing through an area inhabited by the Hunters. The

13

Hunters were indiscriminate when it came to meat and hides. A Lion hide could be sold the same as a Bear hide. Tiger meat was just as tasty as Lion meat. An old hide sold for the same amount as a young hide. Very few days passed when it was not noticed that a Lion or Tiger or Bear did not return to his or her cave as the sun sat low in the sky.

The Hunters over many generations had perfected their hunting methods. They would enter the jungle as the sun was going down and stake out a particular area. When the Lions and Tigers and Bears awoke and started to roam the jungle, the Hunters would be ready and quiet and in a matter of minutes would be dragging their catch towards their huts. Later in the day, there would be much grief in some cave, as it became apparent that yet another Hunter had been successful. Sometimes the Hunters would hide near the watering holes for days awaiting any Lion or Tiger or Bear that would come near. Sometimes they hid in the thick vegetation. When Hunters were about, the kingdom became a very unfriendly place.

Tau and Nono's System

Organizing

Tau and Nono had spoken often about what might be done to remedy this problem. They had a responsibility to do something not simply for themselves, but also for the Tigers and Bears. After all, they were the two that had the name among the Lions. It had never been said but that also meant that they had a great name among the Tigers and the Bears.

Tau and Nono, during one of their meetings came up with a method that just might work. They would organize certain Lions and have them patrol the entire jungle and use their size and fearsome look and their ability to roar to scare the Hunters. If they were scared, then maybe they would not enter the jungle under cover of night. Tau and

Nono reasoned that if they owned the night, then the Hunters would not be able to sneak in after dark and the hunts would end.

It was a tremendous plan and it would take a great deal of courage to carry it out. Nono and Tau started to talk about how they would choose Lions for this very dangerous work. They needed to establish certain rules for selecting 'Pride Lions'. They knew they needed Lions of great courage, but also strength and wisdom. So Tau and Nono established the criteria.

The Criteria

First, a 'Pride Lion' must be 2-7 years old. And of course it went without saying … only males. A 'Pride Lion' must be sound of limb and must have a roar that brought terror to the heart of any Hunter. Tau indicated that a 'Pride Lion' should have a certain bearing and presence. He must have a certain charisma among the other Lions. Tau couldn't exactly explain what bearing, presence and charisma were, but he knew what they looked like when he saw them. Tau was extremely good at determining when there was a lack of bearing, presence or charisma.

Now the look of a 'Pride Lion' was deemed extremely important to his ability to perform this most important work. He must have a thick golden coat of hair. He must have large paws with all claws present and sharp. His mane should be full and three to four shades darker than the coat hair. He must present a very fearsome appearance. It would seldom be necessary for a 'Pride Lion' to fight a Hunter. If his appearance was right, the Hunters should run as soon as they saw him. As a matter of fact, the roar of a true 'Pride Lion' should put a Hunter to flight.

Tau and Nono had each had confrontations with Hunters and had become convinced that those Hunters had run simply because of the way they looked and roared. So it was very important that they choose Lions that looked just like them. Neither Tau nor Nono ever seemed to notice that they looked very similar and that the criteria would almost certainly ensure that they chose 'Pride Lions' that looked just like them.

In addition to these physical characteristics, a 'Pride Lion must be fully trained. Nono thought that in addition to the training that all Lions received in their families, 'Pride Lions' should receive special training to prepare them for the eventuality that they might someday come face to face with a Hunter. He though it might be possible to set up a Pride Lion Academy, a preparatory school for those Lions that would some day become a part of this elite group. Only 'Pride

Lions' would attend and they would spend their time discussing the things they had learned about Hunters and how they do their gruesome work. Tau had once thought that it might be beneficial to allow all Lions to attend. But Nono explained that only those that had a possibility of becoming 'Pride Lions' would even be interested in discussing the Hunters and how to keep them out of the jungle.

Finally, Tau and Nono reasoned that only Lions that were mated could be 'Pride Lions'. A Lion that was single would not have the necessary commitment to stand uncompromisingly in the face of Hunters regardless of their personal fear. A mated Lion would be willing to die to protect his mate and babies. A single Lion might run if things got too dangerous.

The criteria was never divulged by either Nono or Tau to any of the Lions or Tigers or Bears. After all, they had the name among the Lions and that also gave them the name among the Tigers and the Bears. This meant that their decisions were above questioning by anyone.

Performance Assumed

Tau and Nono each returned to their region of the jungle and started selecting those that would be called 'Pride Lions'. Word of this great undertaking swept through the jungle quickly. Soon young Lions were bragging among themselves about all the courage that they must have displayed in the past that helped them during the selection process.

These stories spread through all the Lions and Tigers and Bears. Soon, whenever a 'Pride Lion' walked through the jungle, they were afforded a great deal of esteem. They were met almost with a sense of awe.

Once a Lion was selected, there was an almost immediate assumption that he could perform as a 'Pride Lion'. He had several things in his favor. First, he was selected by the two Lions that had the name among all the Lions. And second, he looked the part.

Roving Patrols – The Only Way

This work would be dangerous business. 'Pride Lions' would be in almost constant contact with the Hunters. 'Pride Lions' used a particular method to secure their region of the jungle. Each 'Pride Lion' was given an assigned route that they would roam. They would look for any indication that a Hunter was in the area. While they walked they would roar at regular intervals. This was to keep the Hunters wondering where they were. The roaring also scared off any approaching Hunters.

When a Hunter was brave enough to enter the jungle, he was quickly identified and then the chase would begin. The 'Pride Lion' would run behind the Hunter almost on his heels. A well-trained 'Pride Lion' would never catch a Hunter. It was more effective to have him return to the plain and tell other would-be Hunters about his terrifying experience. The 'Pride Lions' knew there was great value in these stories. The experience grew larger and more terrifying with each telling.

The 'Pride Lions' were successful immediately. And with each successful patrol, the esteem of the 'Pride Lions' rose. They would sit around their fires at night a tell about the happenings on the patrols. Tigers and Bears and other Lions started to invent explanations about why things were going so well. Some said it was the coloring of the 'Pride Lion'. Maybe it was the roaring that did it. Maybe it was because the 'Pride Lion' had better vision or hearing than the others. Who knew? Maybe it was simply because 'Pride Lions' were smarter or braver than everyone else.

Young Lions dreamed of someday becoming 'Pride Lions'. Young Tigers often pretended they were 'Pride Lions' off on an important patrol. Young Bears would roam around the jungle playing Pride Lions and Hunters. Whenever any young inhabitant of the jungle was asked 'what do you want to be when you grow up' and the answer was 'a Pride Lion' there was a tremendous amount of acceptance and agreement. After all, wasn't the status of 'Pride Lion' the highest level anyone could rise to in the kingdom?

Great Benefits

Because it was such dangerous work, it only seemed right that certain benefits should go to the 'Pride Lions'. So as time went on, 'Pride Lions' started to receive some special benefits. So 'Pride Lions' became the first to eat at a kill and they always ate their fill. Even when game was scarce, the 'Pride Lions' had to receive all the food they needed so they could stay out on patrol protecting everyone in the jungle.

'Pride Lions' were always the first to use the water holes and during drought conditions, the only one to use certain holes. This privilege started innocently at first. The others just simply backed away when a 'Pride Lion' approached just to show appreciation. Later, anyone that continued to drink when a 'Pride Lion' approached received a quick admonishment from those that had shown the proper degree of respect.

'Pride Lions' always received special considerations. With any dealings, they received little extras. It was assumed that they were honest and had the highest values. They were always treated as if they were valuable beyond measure. And they lived lives of high privilege. But then they did risk more and bring more value to the kingdom than others.

Tau and Nono Meet Often

Tau and Nono met often to talk about the activity in their regions. They both knew, even though it was never stated that they were competitors. Each secretly hoped that one day he would have the name among all that lived in the kingdom. Each wanted desperately to out perform the other.

The Difficulty

The situation seemed to get more difficult each day. There always seemed to be fewer and fewer Lions. The Hunters were successful from time to time and managed to take a Lion. But because of the pressure of the never ending patrols, there were just fewer young Lions that could meet the criteria and eventually become 'Pride Lions'.

There seemed to be more Hunters each day. More who were eager to take the risks if only for the off chance that they might gain meat and hide for their efforts.

To compound the problem, there seemed to be more Tigers and Bears each year and that meant there was a great need for more caves. And more caves meant the kingdom was expanding. And a larger kingdom meant a larger area to patrol. This problem had been growing each year but no one had ever come up with a sound idea about how to address the need. It seemed that changing was no longer a 'nice-to-do' option. Devising some method to address these pressing needs had quickly become an imperative.

Mpasa and Ebo Challenge The Process

Mpasa and Ebo's Perspective

Mpasa, the Tiger and Ebo, the Bear were aware of the problem and had talked together often about the possibility of Tigers and Bears taking over some of the responsibilities of the 'Pride Lions'. Mpasa and Ebo were proud and could think of no reason why a Tiger and a Bear weren't as good as any Lion.

Mpasa and Ebo came early one morning to hold council with Tau and Nono. Mpasa sat and looked earnestly at Tau and Nono and spoke with a great deal of confidence and determination.

"We have observed the new challenge that faces us as a kingdom. There are more Hunters everyday and the size of the kingdom continues to expand. And there are fewer Lions to secure the kingdom. We have young Tigers and Bears who could secure the kingdom as well as any Lion."

Tau and Nono were immediately offended. The very idea that Tigers and Bears were equal to Lions. Nono replied, "is it your belief that a Tiger or a Bear could possibly be a 'Pride Lion'?"

Ebo answered "only a Lion could be a 'Pride Lion', but a Bear can do the work of securing the kingdom as well as any Lion".

Tau spoke next. "Can a Tiger or Bear look like a 'Pride Lion'? Can he walk a route and continuously roar to keep any Hunter at bay? Is it possible that you believe that a Tiger or Bear could give chase when he spots a Hunter, never catching him but scaring him enough to keep him and other Hunters from ever entering the jungle again?"

Nono smiled with arrogance.

Ebo answered, "as well as any Lion".

Tau and Nono had discussed what they considered several realistic options but neither of them had even remotely considered the possibility of using Tigers or Bears. After all … they were not Lions. Tau had nothing against Tigers or Bears. He believed that there were some things that Tigers and Bears were particularly good at. But certainly nothing as important as the security of the kingdom.

Nono considered himself a good person, but there was a certain order to things. There were things at which Tigers excelled. The same as Bears. But now here they were proposing that they go against the natural order of things. Nono thought to himself about all the things that Tigers and Bears do that he had never once tried to do himself. If he was good enough to stay out of Tiger and Bear things, why couldn't they stay out of Lion things?

Tau's thoughts turned to how he or Nono would explain to the other Lions that a Tiger or a Bear would be elevated to the same status as a 'Pride Lion'. What would they even be called? 'Pride Tigers ... 'Pride Bears'. He thought about his grandfather, who had given him many of his beliefs about Lions and Tigers and Bears. Grandfather had always explained to him that if he were to one day have the name among all the inhabitants of the kingdom that he would have to be concerned about Tigers and Bears as well as Lions. He would roll over in his grave if he knew this discussion was even going on.

He was supposed to benevolently protect Tigers and Bears, not place them in harms way. Bears especially. They had always appeared happy go lucky creatures that were just not concerned with the serious things of life. Would it even be fair to place them in such a dangerous situation?

Lifting his brow and looking sharply at Mpasa and Ebo, Nono murmured "what you are proposing is not in your nature. It would be unfair to expect any Tiger or Bear to be able to perform at such a level. You have to accept the fact that there are some things that Tigers and Bears are good at and this is simply not one of them."

"Mpasa replied, "we know nothing of the kind. It has been assumed that only Tigers can secure the kingdom. It has never been proved. We want the chance to prove our ability."

Tau cried out "but none of you have been trained to conduct security work. All our young Lions that are selected have completed the necessary training. Have any Tigers or Bears been trained?"

Ebo replied, "of course not, since only Lions are allowed to attend Pride Lion Academy. Give us that chance and we will prove that we are as capable as Lions … if not more so. Or is that your greatest fear? That a Tiger or Bear might excel at security work?"

Now Tau and Nono felt challenged. And any challenge must be accepted or a Lion could lose face. It was Tau who spoke.

"Give us time to consider all you have said and then we will give you a decision. But understand, if we give you a chance and you do not succeed, then this question will be decided for all time."

Mpasa said "we will accept your challenge but let me ask one question. Has a Lion ever failed to perform as a 'Pride Lion'?"

Again insulted Nono answered quietly "yes."

"And did that disqualify Lions for all time?"

No answer was given.

Ebo spoke, "if we succeed, then the criteria will be changed."

Ebo and Mpasa walked off while Tau and Nono sat observing them. Now with more questions than they had before. Tau thought to himself, how could a Bear or Tiger ever do the things that a Lion could do. He had always been taught that Lions were different from Tigers and Bears and in his mind that always meant just a little better. What if Mpasa and Ebo were right? What would become of things then?

The Problem With Tigers and Bears

They Don't Meet The Criteria

"How can we consider this thing?" questioned Nono. "They don't come close to meeting the criteria."

Tau agreed, "the Tigers markings would be too easily seen by the Hunters and they are certainly not as large as Lions. Tigers are big, fat and brown colored when what is really needed is someone who is sleek, muscular and tan. The Hunters would quickly find out where they are and then hunt them down for their meat and hides."

Nono nodded in agreement, "their roar is not nearly as loud as that of a good Lion."

"I have heard that they are very moody," said Tau. "It would be impossible to work with them. They'd force us to change everything." Nono turned his head down and spoke, "well at least they sought of look like Lions, how'd you like to spend the day trying to work with a Bear." "I don't have anything against them, and I suppose they have their place, but performing security work? They weigh far too much to keep up any kind of a decent pace during a patrol. I mean they even look slow. I can't think of a time when I haven't seen them sleep. We'd have to rearrange the schedules to try and make a patrol short enough that they could stay awake." They both laughed.

Nono said "my father told me about a similar situation many years ago. Some older Lions that no longer met the criteria protested and said they could demonstrate that they could still perform a patrol. It was an interesting idea, but after all, rules are rules. Even if an older lion was physically capable of performing properly, everyone knew that their mental ability started to slip as they aged. So how could they possibly be trusted with the security of the entire kingdom?"

Tau said, "I remember those discussions and it was a sad day when some of those old Lions were retired but we must follow the rules or there will be complete chaos." "If we allowed Tigers and Bears to assume the roll of 'Pride Lions', what would be next? Young Lions that want to start before they meet the criteria?" Nono responded "no how about a Lioness trying to scare off a Hunter" The very thought of a lioness performing a security mission was laughable.

Tau said, "the biggest problem is that none of them look like 'Pride Lions'. And the look is really the heart of the effort. Without that look, any Lion or Tiger or Bear could step into the role"

The Perceptions

It's easy to understand how the Lions felt. The Lion culture and value system was very different from the culture and values of Tigers and Bears. Lions were very cooperative by nature. At least with other Lions. Lions were noted for their willingness to share facts. They placed great value on their independence. Lions always connect with each other by doing things with other Lions. From their point of view, there was no reason to connect with anyone else. Once during their lives, most male Lions connect with a particular Lioness but that was primarily a 'Pride Lion' needed to have a mate. And there was also the need to create a male heir that would some day possibly change the fortunes of the entire family by being selected under the criteria as a 'Pride Lion'.

Now Tigers on the other hand share feelings. They always appeared very high strung and edgy to Lions and Bears. They were known for sharing their feelings. And they shared their feelings with everyone. Other Tigers, Lions and Bears. They were passionate and that often appeared as an undesirable trait to both Lions and Bears. Tigers were very competitive and controlling. Certainly un-Lion like behavior.

Bears weren't much better. Bears, like Lions, were fairly cooperative. But unlike Lions, they were far too agreeable. They lacked the kind of stern appearance that was the hallmark of a Lion. Lions valued their independence. Bears valued their interdependence. And if that wasn't bad enough, Bears were always talking. They could spend hours wasting time just talking. For a Lion, after the facts were given, the conversation was over. Bears just talk and talk and talk.

It's Hard Working With "Them"

Tau and Nono were sure that it would be hard working with Tigers and Bears. First of all, it was hard just trying to communicate with Tigers and Bears. With Tigers and Bears, bad is good and lame has nothing to do with and injury. When you work with a Lion, that is just an unspoken understanding of what's going on and how things are done. But now with Tigers and Bears ... It would just be an impossible situation.

Tau thought this might be a solution if they just acted like Lions. He wondered why don't they just act normal ... like us?

Even considering this would cause another problem that would further jeopardize the objective of securing the kingdom. If the most important thing is securing the kingdom, then shouldn't those best qualified to conduct security be left alone to do what they do best?

Visit to Camara *The Teacher*

A decision must be made and when they refused to allow the Tigers and Bears to help, there would be great disagreement that would quickly spread over the entire kingdom. Tau and Nono could think of only one way out. Camara, the Teacher. He was well respected by all that lived in the jungle. Surely Camara would be able to resolve the situation.

Tau and Nono went to the far side of the jungle. They approached the cave of Camara and called into him. Camara walked to the front of his cave and eyed Tau and Nono. He had often heard of these two and their exploits. He had also observed the changes that were occurring in the kingdom and wondered how long it would be before the two of them came to see him.

Camara sat and listened intently to all they had to say. Tau and Nono recounted all that had been said in their meeting with Mpasa and Ebo. They explained the situation and the necessity for making a decision as soon as possible. Camara perceived a that they faced a defining moment in the continuing growth of the kingdom. At this point, the course of future generations could be set for many years to come.

Camara, in a voice made coarse by the years, started to speak to the two young rulers.

"First, Consider What You Believe"

"Biases and beliefs take over and often cloud perceptions. You must constantly consider what you believe. Our beliefs are often inaccurate, colored by our biases and we all have biases.

Preferences for one thing over another. What are yours?

The quicker you release old beliefs, the faster you will develop new beliefs and benefits from those beliefs. You have come to where you are, brought the kingdom to where it is based upon your beliefs and biases. To continue to advance, you must examine and as is often necessary change your beliefs. Keep those that are valid and overcome the rest."

Our biases blind us to the true reality of any situation. In that condition, even when we are confronted with truth, we will consider it false because our biases tell us whatever we see that does not agree with the bias is false. We must constantly ask, what opportunities am I missing because of the biases I maintain.

Tau asks, "where do our biases come from?" Camara continues, "we have a desire to be higher than. Lions desire to be higher than Tigers. Tigers desire to be higher than Bears. Hunters desire to be higher than Lions and Tigers and Bears. I dare say you two desire to be higher than me."

Tau and Nono quickly cast their gaze towards the ground.

Camara assured them. "It is a very natural desire. We must ensure that the desire to be higher than does not interfere with the thing that must be accomplished. But as we evolve, we must at some time give up the desire to be higher than others."

"Old patterns of bias and belief must be challenged. We must be vigilant when it comes to reexamining our conventional thinking

"We Must See The Possibilities"

"There is a need to get as many involved in all aspects of your operation as possible. The more that are involved, the easier it is for all. There is greater profitability if there is greater performance and there is greater performance if more participate.

We must recognize our collective interdependence. We are all very independent but we are also connected one to another. So to truly succeed, we must all succeed. For all to succeed, we must recognize our individual uniqueness. We are all different but connected. Much as your tail is connected to you just like your paw. Each very important. Each providing a very different function.

To determine the best way to profit from individual uniqueness, we must remember to observe and listen. The best way is to work together and pay attention to each other. We must learn each other's language and customs and values. Then we will function better together.

"FEAR Makes Us Do What We Would Not Do"

"We fear doing those things that go beyond our comfort zone. We do some things one way for so long that it becomes comfortable and then we fear changing. Observation comes to an end when we become comfortable. Without constant observation, we are unprepared for inevitable changes.

Fear journeys with us when we travel from the comfortable to the uncomfortable. When we are uncomfortable, we avoid making decisions because decisions are risky and risky leads to more fear. Fear causes paralysis. It makes cowards of us. We must override our desire for comfort. It will cause us to lose our desire to explore and do better.

"Develop A Different Paradigm"

Remember that there are always at least two perspectives … probably more. Consider why have you chosen your particular perspective? And then find another way of looking at the situation"

Tau and Nono were considering all that Camara was saying. But there was a need to issue some warnings. Camara gave them a warning by saying…

"Expect Resistance To Change"

"Those you lead will resist 'different' because different causes us to leave our comfort zone. Most see little value in 'different'. Accepting and valuing differences of thought and people leads to positive outcomes.

We must constantly look for ways to remove barriers that prevent some from contributing to the group's success using their own unique performance position. But accepting that this is possible comes slowly. Expect resistance to come constantly. There will be conflict and you must address it every time it comes up. You will be inviting some that have been historically locked out to participate. Those that have always been invited historically will react believing that changing is always a mistake. Acceptance comes slowly and often ... painfully.

And when you find behavior that is not in keeping with the new values ... confront it using the new values. Tell them simply – we don't do that here."

"Tell Them 'What To Do' Not 'How To Do'"

Accept the fact that new team members will perform tasks differently. They have a different culture and think differently so they will approach tasks from their point of view not yours. After all, your methods are not the methods that have always been used. Your responsibility is to provide the support that allows each new team member to succeed by using their uniqueness to the benefit of the team. You must integrate a multitude of diverse styles. It's possible. Difficult! But possible. The ones that make the effort to become proficient style integrators will find incredible success. While those who withdraw from all the hard work that will be required will find themselves forever performing at a mediocre level.

Examine Beliefs and Change

Camara, when he was finished his comments, simply arose and walked back into his cave.

Tau and Nono sat for a moment thinking about all they had heard. The words had a ring of truth to them but they also presented them with more problems than they had come with.

Consider what you believe
See the possibilities
Fear makes us do what we would not do
Develop a different paradigm
Expect resistance to change
Tell them what to do, not how to do

To do the things that Camara suggested they would have to change the way things were being done. It was true that something had to be done, but this was *their system.* They, in their infinite wisdom, had defined and implemented this system. To change it might give the appearance that they had made a mistake when it was first designed. What would happen to their esteem if they made changes such as these?

Nono Holds His Beliefs

Nono thought for awhile. He weighed the comfort of his current position against the risks of taking these steps. If he allowed this, what might be next? Sure there were possibilities. But did the possibility for gain outweigh the possibility for loss. How could he admit that a system that he had designed could be done better? If Tigers and Bears were equal to Lions, couldn't that mean that 'Pride Lions' were equal to Him? How would he rule if his authority was compromised? This was too much.

After all, the situation might simply correct itself. Suppose the kingdom stays at its current size. Then we would only need a few more 'Pride Lions' to maintain the same level of security that they had always had.

"We add a few more patrols and extend the actual time a little and we'll be all right until we have some more 'Pride Lions' to help out. Yes, we'll keep things the same. If my beliefs must be changed, then my beliefs are wrong. If my beliefs are wrong … then what does that say about me? Yes, we'll keep things the same. That will be better for all concerned. Yes, we'll keep things the same. We have established a tradition here and tradition is important. I don't see Tigers or Bears giving up any of their traditions. Yes, we'll keep things the same. The same is better.

Nono held on to his beliefs and nothing changed among his 'Pride Lions'. To Nono's surprise things got worse. But he held to his beliefs and continued to tell his Lions to redouble their efforts and things would get better.

Tau Examines His Beliefs and Dreams

Tau thought about what Camara had said.

"Biases and beliefs take over and often cloud perceptions. You must constantly consider what you believe." Did he have biases that were blinding him to an obvious solution to the problem? He remembered Camara saying "we have a desire to be higher than others. It is a very natural desire." Tau knew beyond a shadow of a doubt that he did in fact desire to have the name among all the inhabitants of the kingdom. What if Camara was right? What if there was a level of performance that he had not even considered yet? Worst case was that if he tried and it failed, he could look as if he was willing to do anything to protect the kingdom.

What did he really believe? He believed what he had been told. Only Lions can provide security for the kingdom. And there is only one way to conduct security … rove, roar and chase. Those that provide security deserve special benefits from the rest the kingdom. And there will always be enough Lions.

But now, there were not enough Lions, so that was no longer a valid belief. If that was not a valid belief, what about the others? Could Tigers and Bears provide security as well as a Lion? Could they do it better? Was it possible to perform security in some way different from the way Lions had always done it?

He knew from his own experience that the quicker he released old beliefs, the faster he would develop new beliefs and benefits from those beliefs. This problem would not simply go away by itself. Something had to be done and if that required a personal change on his part, he was willing. He had to keep in mind what was most important. He was willing to challenge old patterns of bias and belief and then be vigilant when it came to reexamining his conventional thinking.

Tau thought, is what I believe true considering these circumstances? Because of the blindness caused by my biases, have I been selecting only those who look just like me every time!

Suppose he could create and maintain an environment that capitalizes on all the gifts, skills, perspectives and talents available "using everything and everyone available". Tau started to get excited as he sold himself on these new beliefs. Sure there is greater profitability if there is greater performance and there is greater performance if more participate.

He could create a collaborative environment that brings together the talents and experiences of everyone to individually and collectively produce better ideas and superior results. What is the potential inherent in this individual because of their gifts, talents, skills and perspective? How can they be most beneficial?

Tau Makes Changes

Tau called all his 'Pride Lions' together. As they approached, it became apparent that this would be no ordinary gathering. Mpasa and Ebo walked with him. Tau had planned to give the speech of a lifetime. As the last 'Pride Lion' took his place, Tau began.

"We all know the problems we face. If we continue doing what we have been doing, we can only expect to get what we've been getting. If we continue thinking what we've been thinking, we'll continue doing what we've been doing. We must change. And the quicker we change the better. I have decided that we will change. We will be different. Because nothing is more important than the kingdom and all the inhabitants of the kingdom. It is for these reasons that Tigers and Bears will be trained and used to secure the kingdom."

The roar was almost deafening. Tau stood his ground. He held his composure as he had on so many previous occasions. He waited until the roaring ended, and then spoke.

"I understand that for some this is not a popular decision. And there are other decisions that could be made, but this is my decision. It is a risky decision and there will be challenges to overcome because of it. But it has always been my desire that we be the very best we can be … not simply adequate."

"It is not enough for us to be good or even successful. We must improve and improve until we are the very best we can be. We must have new beliefs and we must know that we can. So I ask you all to consider what you believe. Determine if your beliefs are valid.

The quicker you release old beliefs, the faster you will develop new beliefs and benefit from those beliefs. Old patterns of bias and belief must be challenged.

We must recognize our collective interdependence. We are all connected one to another. So to truly succeed, we must all succeed. For all to succeed, we must recognize our individual uniqueness. To determine the best way to use individual uniqueness, we must remember to observe and listen. The best way is to work together and pay attention to each other. We must learn each other's language and customs and values. Then we will function better together.

Remember that there are always at least two perspectives ... probably more. Consider why have you chosen your particular perspective? And then find another way of looking at the situation.

We can do this. We will do this. I expect our best effort."

And Then ...

Lions Resist The Change

The Lions slowly started to leave. Some still voiced their disagreement. Some seemed upset about how this change might effect them personally. The roaring continued late into the night. It was the topic of discussion among all the Lions.

But it was also the topic of discussion among all the Tigers and the Bears. There was disagreement there also. Tigers and Bears understood the consequences of this event. They understood the dangers. Not all the Tigers or Bears thought this was a good thing. There were many that thought that maintaining the security of the kingdom was something that was best left to those most qualified. Lions.

Mpasa and Ebo listened as Tigers and Bears murmured and complained about the changes. Some of them didn't want the changes any more than some of the Lions. But change came anyway.

Ebo Gets Great Results

Ebo started to patrol just as the lions patrolled. The constant walking was difficult but he did it anyway. He kept in mind that this was important and that future Bears would benefit from his efforts. He roamed his assigned route and when a Hunter approached, he roared and chased. Soon he was getting a name among the Lions. Soon, some of the Lions changed their opinions ... but only about Ebo.

During a discussion one-day, several of the Lions were talking to Ebo. They had come to respect him and his ability.

"You're not like the rest of them. As a matter of fact, you're more like a Lion than a Bear."

Ebo stood and simply walked away. The Lions were not sure what had happened or why Ebo suddenly left.

Mpasa Struggles

Mpasa started to patrol just as the lions patrolled. The constant walking was difficult for him, but he did it anyway. He kept in mind that this was important and that future Tigers would benefit from his efforts. He roamed his assigned route and when a Hunter approached, he roared and chased.

Mpasa's results were less impressive than Ebo's. Less impressive than the Lions'. Hunters sometimes got past him. There were times when he tired so much from the constant walking that he was not quite as attentive as he could have been. Mpasa redoubled his efforts with very limited results.

Tau observed this and knew that all the Tigers would be judged by Mpasa's performance. Then, Tau remembered Camara's words … "Tell them 'what to do' not 'how to do." Accept the fact that new team members will perform tasks differently. They have a different culture and think differently so they will approach tasks from their point of view. Your responsibility is to provide the support that allows each to succeed by using their uniqueness to the benefit of the team. You must integrate a multitude of diverse styles.

Tau asked, "I need to ensure that no Hunter ever enters any part of the kingdom that you are securing, how can you do that?"

Mpasa thought and said, "It would be better if I stayed in one place and used my sense of smell to spot approaching Hunters. If I then sprint across the jungle, especially at night, they will think there are Tigers all over the place. After a few weeks, you could even cut down on the number of patrols. As a matter of fact, I believe my eyesight is better than most Lions. I would prefer to patrol at night and never left Hunters into the jungle."

Tau thought about it for a moment. "Let's try it that way."

There Once Was A Lion, A Tiger and A Bear ...

Tau was moving through the jungle one morning and overheard three Lions talking.

"There once was a Lion and a Tiger and a Bear. And…" As Tau listened, he remembered the words of Camara.

"Expect Resistance To Change. Those you lead will resist 'different' because different causes us to leave our comfort zone. Most see little value in 'different'. Accepting and valuing differences of thought and people leads to positive outcomes.

There will be conflict and you must address it every time it comes up. When you find behavior that is not in keeping with the new values … confront it using the new values. Tell them simply – we don't do that here."

Tau approached the three Lions. Seeing him, they started the story again. Tau interrupted. "Is this story one you would tell if Tigers and Bears were here?"

"Of course not."

"Then understand … we don't do that here."

The Lions dropped their heads and soon wandered off.

Tau Wonders

Tau was satisfied with the results. The criteria was changed. Tigers and Bears would be included as candidates in the future. They would work using their unique skills and talents. This would be risky. However, it would ensure that the most important thing, protecting the kingdom, would be treated as the most important thing. Not allowing biases and old beliefs to become more important than the most important thing.

Why Had He Never Considered The Possibilities

He was quickly discovering that when you start getting all your diversity involved in the game, you become unstoppable; profiting from your diversity. Not that there weren't problems. There was always something. Resistance by the Lions. Complaints by Tigers and Bears. Misunderstandings. Always something but slowly but surely their performance started to improve.

Tau had discovered that the responsibility for initiating inclusion lies everyone. The Lions had to get Tigers and Bears playing. Tigers and Bears needed to do their part. Their responsibility was to perform at the top of their abilities. Mpasa needed to consider his performance so he knew how to respond when he discussed his performance with Tau. Tau needed to have the courage to tell Mpasa that there was a problem.

Just One Big Happy Family

Tau contemplated the situation and what he now believed. He was sure now that Camara was correct when he said that biases will always exist. He was sure that the Lions and Tigers and Bears would probably never be one big happy family. The differences caused by culture, age, values, experiences, personality, education and others might always exist. But now, Tau wondered if the fact that these things would always exist was a problem after all.

Lessons Learned

Tau and The Lions of The South

Tau and the Lions of the south had learned several things from the experience. A diverse workforce, at every level, is a valuable resource for creating competitive advantage. A culture that enables team members to operate comfortably with a variety of perspectives strengthens the team's capacity to learn from each other and deal with arising issues.

Building an inclusive environment will improve performance while capitalizing on cultural differences.

Including as many as possible in the effort is the thing to do. Not because it is the fair thing to do and not because it is the moral thing to do. But because it is the profitable thing to do.

Tau was also convinced that it was much better to make decisions faster. Acting is better than reacting.

As Tau considered how his fortunes had improved, he wondered how Nono was making out. But he had noticed that he was patrolling more and more of the kingdom each and every day. His name was growing.

NEW VALUES IN 'THE KINGDOM

Tau continued to make speeches, make difficult decisions and take the high ground in any and every discussion. Lions and Tigers and Bears eventually learned that it is profitable to…

Work toward common goals

Act as if the 'important thing' really is the 'important thing'

Look for ways to make diversity work

Help each other win and take pride in each victory

Realize that being right is irrelevant to good performance

Perception matters

Develop and maintain a commitment to improvement

Embrace the diversity of your team members with a positive approach and an attitude that integrates uniqueness

Refuse to live beneath potential

Finally

And it came to pass

Tau visited Camara once again to tell him of the great changes made in his region. Camara is pleased. Tau asks "why did you not tell previous generations how to work together to accomplish more?"

Camara takes a deep breath and looks towards the ground. "I did, but their blindness was too great. They were not ready. It has been written, "the saddest words of tongue or pen are the ones that list…what might have been"

The kingdom continued to expand and more Hunters came to hunt. Nono held to his beliefs. Even in the face of continuing pressure and more and more growth under Tau. Tau was quite happy

78

and pleased with himself. He continued to prepare himself for any change that might come in the future. A good thing too.

Because as he was sitting in his cave early one morning, Hafsah, a Lioness approached to hold council with Tau. She sat and looked earnestly at Tau and spoke with a great deal of confidence and determination. And said...

"We have observed the new challenge that faces us as a kingdom. There are more Hunters everyday and the size of the kingdom continues to expand. And even with more Lions and Tigers and Bears the challenge will continue to grow. We have young female Lions and Tigers and Bears who could secure the kingdom as well as any male."

Tau smiled and thought about better performance and having the name among all in the kingdom.

As you complete this parable

And contemplate what you will do next remember ...

Discover and understand that there is profitability in differences

Develop a high tolerance for debate and conflict

Endeavor to exploit uniqueness

Affirm uniqueness as valuable

Develop and maintain the expectation that all team members can and must contribute

Practice zero tolerance for activity and behavior that installs barriers

Affirm the belief that everyone is responsible for inclusion

I'd Like Others To Gain This Insight

To order additional copies of this book call Art
Jackson Seminars at: 703-680-3203
For More Information About Books, Study Materials
and Art Jackson Presentations
Please call   703-680-3203
Or write us   artjackson@usa.net
Or visit   www.artjackson.com
Or write: Art Jackson Seminars 14540 Colony Creek
Ct. Woodbridge, VA 22193

This book is available at special quantity discounts.

No cash/CODs. Fax orders to 703-730-0413. Please
allow 4-6 weeks for US delivery.

This offer is subject to change without notice.

Who Is Art Jackson

The author, Art Jackson Art Jackson is a nationally recognized and respected leader, speaker and author whose insights have helped hundreds of his clients discover and manifest their intended level of greatness.

Art has been referred to as an expert in leadership with over 25 years of formal leadership education and 15 years in leadership and management positions in the military and in corporations.

He is a graduate of the United States Military Academy at West Point and Lesley College in Cambridge, Massachusetts. Art holds a Bachelor of Science degree in Engineering, a Master of

Science degree in Management and is continuing his studies towards a Master of Theology degree.

Art has been a speaker and trainer in Korea, Canada, Japan, Egypt and all across the United States delivering seminars on personal leadership, team building and diversity and inclusion. He has presented keynote addresses for Fortune 500 companies, government agencies, churches and schools.

Mr. Jackson brings a new perspective to diversity and inclusion work. His military background brings a very focused perspective that keeps him looking at two things. Mission first - People always. It is the mission that is most important and anything that gets in the way of the mission is to be overcome by any means necessary. People are the means by which the mission is accomplished, so any barrier to people performing at their very best is to be overcome by any means necessary. To the question, "which is most important, the mission or the people?", Art's answer is always "yes." The mission can not be accomplished without the people. And people can only prosper when the mission is accomplished. When we look at equal employment opportunity, affirmative action, diversity and inclusion from that prospective, we will se that everyone must play and play well. Everyone must use their own unique capabilities to maximum advantage to get the mission accomplished. Everyone must profit from the accomplishment of the mission.

Mr. Jackson is a member of the National Speakers Association, the National Capital Speakers Association, and the Les Brown 2000 Organization.

Bookmark

[Lions and Tigers and Bears logo watermark]

From the bestseller

Lions and Tigers and Bears – Oh My
A Parable Of Diversity And Inclusion/Art Jackson

Copyright © January 2001 by Art Jackson

For More Information About Books, Study Materials
and Art Jackson Presentations
Please call   703-680-3203
Or write us   artjackson@usa.net
Or visit   www.artjackson.com

-

Art Jackson

About the Author

The author, Art Jackson Art Jackson is a graduate of the United States Military Academy at West Point and Lesley College in Cambridge, Massachusetts. Art holds a Bachelor of Science degree in Engineering, a Master of Science degree in Management and is continuing his studies towards a Master of Theology degree.

Art has been a speaker and trainer in Korea, Canada, Japan, Egypt and all across the United States delivering seminars on personal leadership, team building and diversity and inclusion. He has presented keynote addresses for Fortune 500 companies, government agencies, churches and schools.

Mr. Jackson brings a new perspective to diversity and inclusion work. His military background brings a very focused perspective that keeps him looking at two things. Mission first - People always. It is the mission that is most important and anything that gets in the way of the mission is to be overcome by any means necessary. People are the means by which the mission is accomplished, so any barrier to people performing at their very best is to be overcome by any means necessary. To the question, "which is most important, the mission or the people?", Art's answer is always "yes." The mission can not be accomplished without the people. And people can only prosper when the mission is accomplished. When we look at equal employment opportunity, affirmative action, diversity and inclusion from that prospective, we will se that everyone must play and play well. Everyone must use their own unique capabilities to maximum advantage to get the mission accomplished. Everyone must profit from the accomplishment of the mission.

Mr. Jackson is a member of the National Speakers Association, the National Capital Speakers Association, and the Les Brown 2000 Organization.

Printed in the United States
49358LVS00001B/76-177